Favorite Classics for Piano

Arranged by Edwin McLean, John Nicholas and David Pearl

Cherry Lane Music Company
Director of Publications/Project Editor: Mark Phillips
Manager of Publications: Gabrielle Fastman

ISBN: 978-1-60378-042-1

Visit our website at www.cherrylane.com

CONTENTS

Adagio

By Alessandro Marcello
Trans. by Johann Sebastian Bach

Adagio (♪ = ca. 66)

Air

By Wolfgang Amadeus Mozart

Allegretto

Adagio
from WATER MUSIC SUITE

By George Frideric Handel

Air on the G String

from ORCHESTRAL SUITE NO. 3

By Johann Sebastian Bach

Slowly

Allegro

By William Boyce

Allegro Maestoso

from WATER MUSIC

By George Frideric Handel

Allegretto

Ave Maria

By Franz Schubert

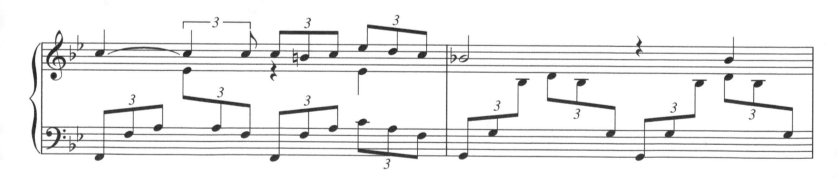

Ave Verum Corpus

(Jesu, Word of God Incarnate)

By Wolfgang Amadeus Mozart

Moderately slow

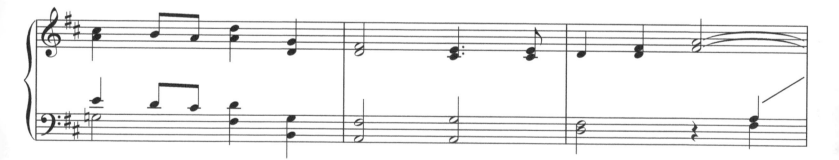

rit.

Be Thou with Me

By Johann Sebastian Bach

Moderately slow

rit.

Canon in D

By Johann Pachelbel

Caro mio ben

Music by Tommaso Giordani

Moderately slow

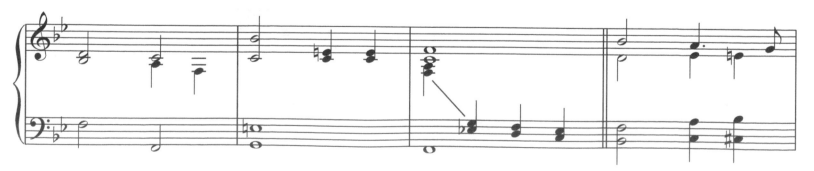

Slowly   **Tempo I**

Dance of the Spirits

from ORFEO ED EURIDICE

By Christoph Willibald von Gluck

Moderately slow

Fine

D.C. (no repeat) al Fine

Hornpipe

By George Frideric Handel

Allegretto

Elegie
from LES ERINNYES

By Jules Massenet

dim. e rit.

Hallelujah Chorus

from THE MESSIAH

By George Frideric Handel

Intermezzo

from *CAVALLERIA RUSTICANA*

By Pietro Mascagni

mf

with pedal

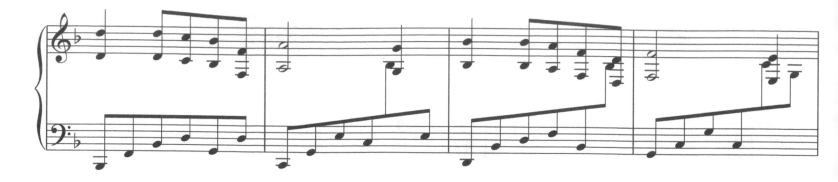

rit. e dim.

p

Jerusalem

By C. H. Parry

44

Jesu, Joy of Man's Desiring

By Johann Sebastian Bach

Andante cantabile

48

Largo

from PIANO CONCERTO IN F MINOR

By Johann Sebastian Bach

Moderately slow

p

Larghetto

By George Frideric Handel

Largo
from XERXES

By George Frideric Handel

Moderately slow

Laudate Dominum
from VESPERAE SOLENNES

By Wolfgang Amadeus Mozart

Slowly, in 1

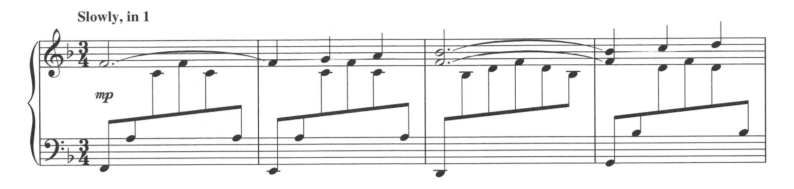

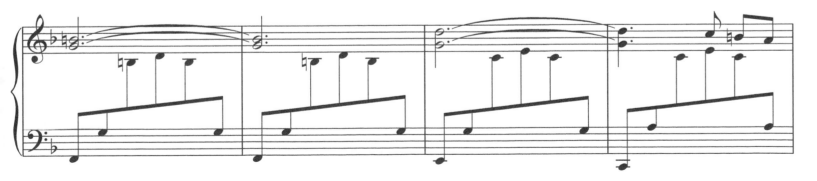

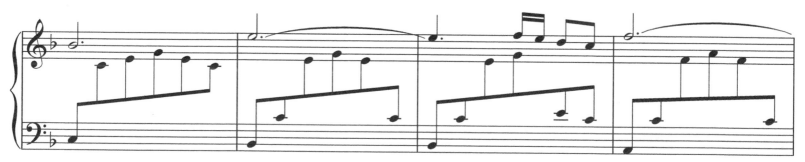

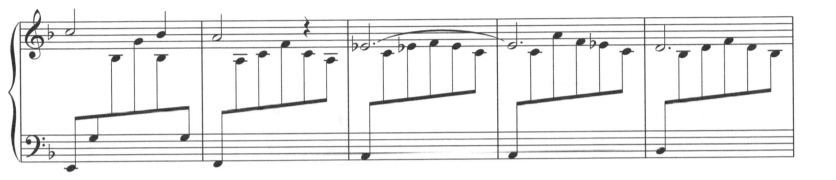

March

By George Frideric Handel

60

Minuet
from ANNA MAGDALENA NOTEBOOK

By Johann Sebastian Bach

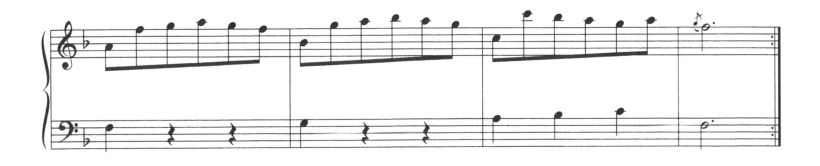

Minuet
from STRING QUARTET

By Luigi Boccherini

Ode to Joy

from SYMPHONY NO. 9 IN D MINOR, FOURTH MOVEMENT CHORAL THEME

Music by Ludwig van Beethoven

Pavane

By Gabriel Fauré

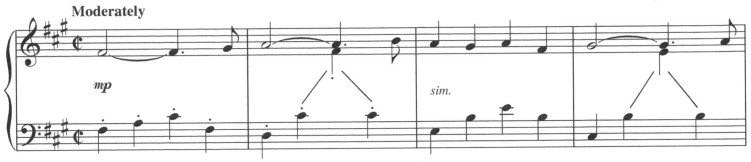

To Coda

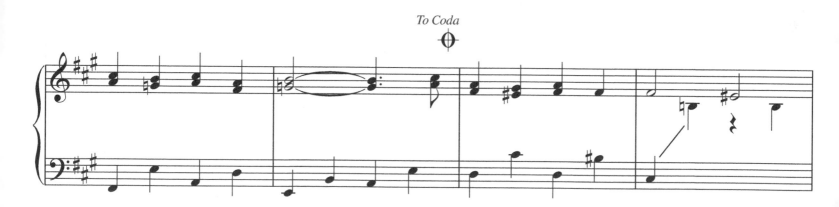

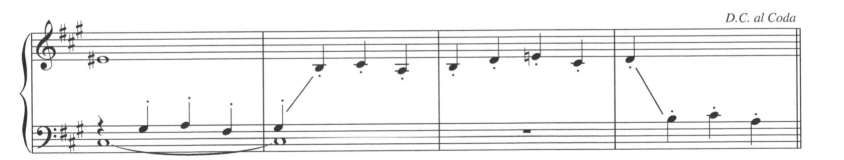

69

Panis Angelicus
(O Lord Most Holy)

By César Franck

Moderately slow

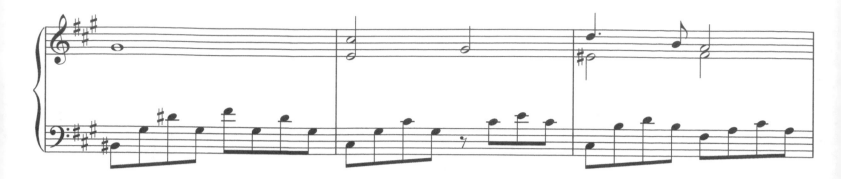

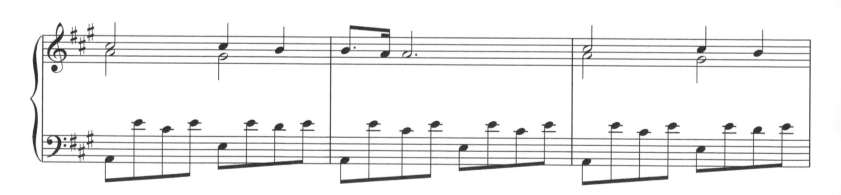

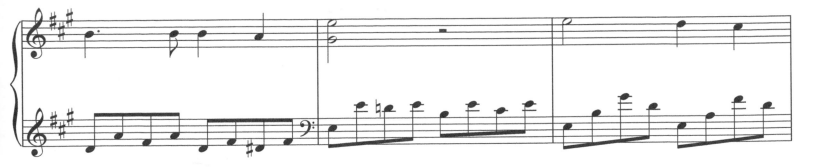

73

Pavane for a Dead Princess

By Maurice Ravel

Moderately slow

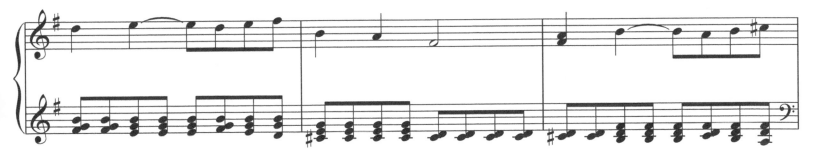

75

Prelude in C
from THE WELL-TEMPERED CLAVIER, PART I

By Johann Sebastian Bach

Sarabande in D Minor

By George Frideric Handel

Rondeau

By Jean-Joseph Mouret

Majestically (Not Fast)

Sarabande in E Minor

By George Frideric Handel

Grave

Sheep May Safely Graze

from CANTATA NO. 208

By Johann Sebastian Bach

rit.

Sinfonia
from CHRISTMAS ORATORIO

By Johann Sebastian Bach

Spring

from THE FOUR SEASONS

By Antonio Vivaldi

Sleepers, Wake

(Wachet Auf)
from CANTATA NO. 140

By Johann Sebastian Bach

Symphony No. 3
Third Movement Theme

By Johannes Brahms

Symphony No. 5
Second Movement

By Franz Schubert

Moderately

Winter
from THE FOUR SEASONS

By Antonio Vivaldi

Theme from Romeo and Juliet

By Pyotr Il'yich Tchaikovsky

Andante cantabile

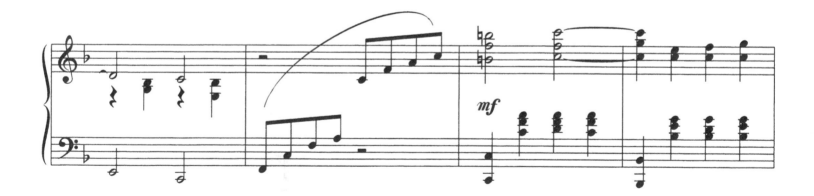

cresc. poco a poco